American Moments

ABDO
Daughters

# THE ASSASSINATION
# OF ROBERT F. KENNEDY

By Rachel A. Koestler-Grack

LOS ANGELES
Ambassador hotel

Kennedy

# VISIT US AT
# WWW.ABDOPUB.COM

Published by ABDO Publishing Company, 4940 Viking Drive, Suite 622, Edina, Minnesota 55435. Copyright © 2005 by Abdo Consulting Group, Inc. International copyrights reserved in all countries. No part of this book may be reproduced in any form without written permission from the publisher. ABDO & Daughters™ is a trademark and logo of ABDO Publishing Company.

Printed in the United States.

Edited by: Melanie A. Howard
Interior Production and Design: Terry Dunham Incorporated
Cover Design: Mighty Media
Photos: AP/Wideworld, Corbis, Library of Congress

**Library of Congress Cataloging-in-Publication Data**

Koestler-Grack, Rachel A., 1973-
    The assassination of Robert F. Kennedy / Rachel A. Koestler-Grack.
        p. cm. --  (American moments)
    Includes index.
    ISBN 1-59197-931-5
    1. Kennedy, Robert F., 1925-1968--Assassination--Juvenile literature.  I. Title. II. Series.

E840.8.K4K64 2005
973.923'092--dc22

                                                                    2004055422

# CONTENTS

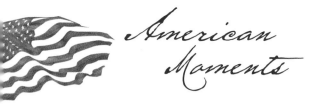
# FROM TRIUMPH TO TRAGEDY

June 4, 1968, was an exciting day in California. It was the day of the California primary. In a primary election, voters from the Democratic, Republican, and other political parties nominate a presidential candidate for their party. The California primary was an important election for Democratic senator Robert F. Kennedy. Only a week before, his Democratic contender, Eugene McCarthy, had won the Oregon primary.

Kennedy relaxed at the home of family friend and filmmaker John Frankenheimer in Malibu, California. Kennedy was finally feeling better after a long, difficult campaign. He considered not attending his own election party at the Los Angeles Ambassador Hotel. Instead, he suggested that his family and friends watch the primary results on television. He even invited the media to join them.

However, the television networks refused to haul their equipment all the way out to Malibu. Therefore, Kennedy agreed to go to Los Angeles. At 7:15 PM, Senator Kennedy and his campaign staff drove to the Ambassador Hotel to await the election returns.

Meanwhile, 24-year-old Sirhan Bishara Sirhan spent the day at the San Gabriel Valley Gun Club in Duarte, California. Throughout the

*Opposite page: Robert F. Kennedy gives his victory speech at the Ambassador Hotel. Standing beside him is his wife, Ethel.*

LOS ANGELES
Ambassador Hotel

Kennedy

afternoon, he fired 300 to 400 rounds at a target with his .22-caliber Iver Johnson revolver. The range supervisor commented that he seemed to be an expert shot. During six hours of practice, Sirhan wore out the center of his target.

At 5:00 PM, Sirhan left the club and got into a run-down, pink-and-white, 1956 Chrysler DeSoto. With his revolver in the car, Sirhan drove to Pasadena, California. He lived there with his Jordanian mother and two brothers. On his way home, he met a friend at Bob's Big Boy restaurant. There, the two young men drank coffee and discussed horse racing. At about 7:15 PM, Sirhan went back to his car. Instead of going home, he drove to the Ambassador Hotel.

At the hotel, campaign aides paced around the Kennedy suite. Around 11:00 PM, the primary results appeared to favor Kennedy. In his room, Kennedy jotted down notes for a speech to give downstairs after the election.

Before long, victory became clear. Kennedy took the freight elevator down to the kitchen. He walked through the pantry into the Embassy Ballroom. Kennedy was greeted by wild cheers from a crowd of supporters. He stepped onto a platform surrounded by 1,800 excited fans. His wife, Ethel, stood beside him.

"I would hope now that the California primary is finished," Kennedy said, "we can now concentrate . . . on what direction we want to go in the United States. . . . around the rest of the globe . . . and whether we're going to continue the policies which have been so unsuccessful in Vietnam. . . . I think we should move in a different direction." Looking out into the crowd, he concluded, "So my thanks

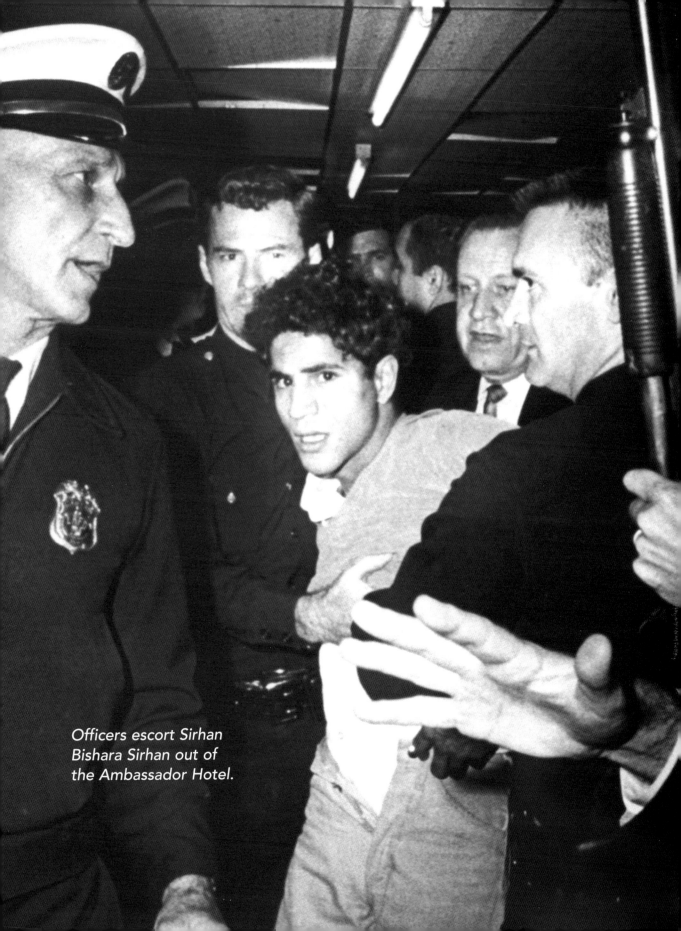

Officers escort Sirhan
Bishara Sirhan out of
the Ambassador Hotel.

## JUNE 4–6, 1968

**11:15 PM, June 4**
Robert F. Kennedy goes down to the Embassy Ballroom of the Ambassador Hotel to give his acceptance speech.

**12:15 AM, June 5**
Kennedy leaves the Embassy Ballroom and heads into the pantry. He is shot by Sirhan Bishara Sirhan.

**12:22 AM, June 5**
Police arrive at the Ambassador Hotel and arrest Sirhan.

**2:15 AM, June 5**
After Sirhan repeatedly refuses to tell police his name, he is finally booked as "John Doe."

**9:35 AM, June 5**
Sirhan's brother, Adel, goes to the police station to identify Sirhan.

**1:44 AM, June 6**
Kennedy dies at Good Samaritan Hospital.

to all of you. And now it's on to Chicago and let's win there!" This victory was just what the Kennedy campaign needed. Many thought he was on the road to the presidency.

Kennedy stepped off the platform. It was just after midnight. Headwaiter Karl Uecker helped clear a path in front of Kennedy. The crowd was thick. Reporters, friends, and others in the audience crowded around the senator. Uecker held Kennedy's arm as they worked their way into the pantry. For a moment, Kennedy broke loose to shake hands with a kitchen worker.

Sirhan was among the crowd gathered outside the Embassy Ballroom. From the pantry, he watched Kennedy come closer. Sirhan then began pushing his way toward Kennedy. When Kennedy was just a few feet away, Sirhan suddenly pulled out his revolver and opened fire.

Senator Kennedy lurched forward then fell backward. Screams erupted in the room. Uecker quickly grabbed

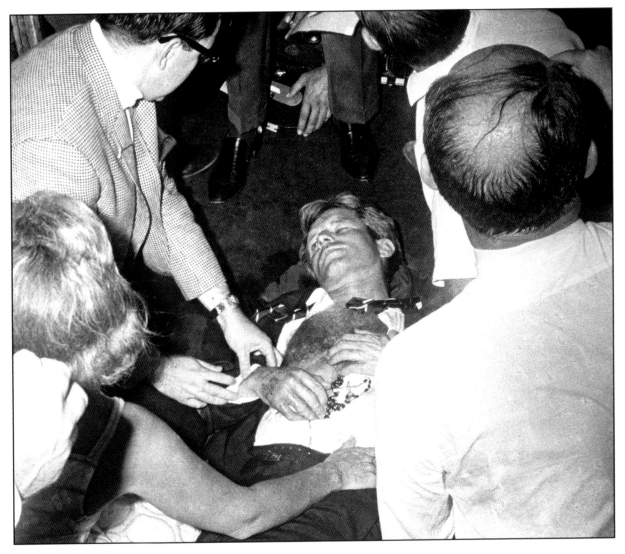

*Ethel Kennedy kneels next to Robert as he lies
wounded on the Ambassador Hotel's pantry floor.*

Sirhan's arm and wrestled with him. But Sirhan continued to pull
the trigger until all of his bullets were spent. Eventually, Uecker and
several others pinned Sirhan down on a nearby table.

Frightened people ran in every direction, trampling balloons and
knocking each other down. Some people simply collapsed to the
ground in shock. By the time Sirhan had finished firing, six people
were wounded, including Senator Kennedy.

# YOUNG BOBBY

Robert Francis Kennedy was born in Brookline, Massachusetts, on November 20, 1925. He was the seventh of nine children of Joseph P. and Rose Kennedy. Few people would have guessed that Bobby would grow up to be a leader. As a child, he was soft-spoken. He earned average grades in school.

Growing up, Robert felt his older brothers, Joseph Jr. and John, received more attention from his parents. They considered John an intellectual. Joseph Sr. hoped Joseph Jr. would become the first Irish Catholic president of the United States.

Things did not go exactly as the Kennedys planned. Joseph Jr. served as a naval pilot in World War II. In August 1944, he flew a secret mission over the English Channel. During the mission, he died when his bomber plane exploded. In 1948, Robert's sister, Kathleen, also died in a plane accident in southern France.

Out of the tragedies, Robert grew strong and focused. Like his brothers, he felt a deep love and commitment to his country. Several months after Joseph Jr.'s death, Robert traveled to Washington DC. He persuaded the secretary of the U.S. Navy to assign him as a seaman to the USS *Joseph P. Kennedy, Jr.* The destroyer was newly named in honor of his brother. He served on the ship from February to May 1946 and then returned to college.

Kennedy graduated from Harvard University in 1948. On June 17, 1950, he married Ethel Skakel. Over their 18-year marriage, the couple had 11 children. In 1951, Kennedy graduated from the University of Virginia Law School.

After graduation, Kennedy began his political career by managing his brother John's successful campaign for the U.S. Senate. In 1953, he earned his own political spot as assistant counsel to the U.S. Senate Permanent Subcommittee on Investigations. The committee was headed by Senator Joseph McCarthy. On the committee, Kennedy helped investigate certain public figures suspected of being communists.

*The Kennedy family in 1935. In the front row* (left to right) *are Jean, Edward, Robert, Kathleen, and Patricia. In the back row* (left to right) *are Eunice, Joseph Sr., Rose, and John. Rosemary and Joseph Jr. are not pictured.*

At this time, many Americans feared communism. McCarthy used this public sentiment to his advantage. Although McCarthy was never able to support any of his claims, the public accepted his accusations. If McCarthy accused someone of being communist, the public immediately decided that the person was guilty.

There seemed to be no way around his charges. A person who used their Fifth Amendment right to not answer a question was labeled a "Fifth Amendment Communist."

The accused were also expected to talk about the communist connections of their friends. McCarthy used the press to humiliate

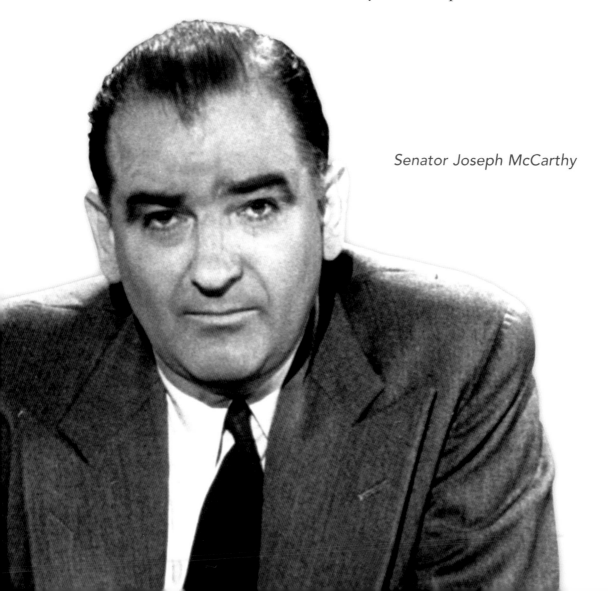

*Senator Joseph McCarthy*

# BLACKLISTING

Americans had been uneasy about communism since the early twentieth century. They saw how easily the Nazis were able to use the media to control the German people in World War II. Many began to wonder if the American media was feeding communist messages to the public. This fear led to an investigation of the movie industry based in Hollywood, California.

Organizations such as the American Legion later threatened to boycott Hollywood movies. Threatened with this possibility, the heads of many studios met in New York in November 1947. The studio heads decided not to hire communists.

Actors Lauren Bacall and Humphrey Bogart protest the treatment of actors.

Businesses checked the backgrounds of actors, writers, and other people who worked in the media. One such company was called American Business Consultants (ABC). In 1950, ABC published an anti-communist list in a booklet called Red Channels. This booklet soon became a blacklisting guide.

Many media workers in Red Channels found themselves out of a job with little hope of ever being hired again. To get their names off of the blacklist, media professionals paid large sums of money to a company called Aware. Blacklisting ended in 1963, when broadcaster and storyteller John Henry Faulk won a lawsuit against Aware.

people.  This public scorn often made people accused by the committee lose their jobs.

Kennedy did not agree with McCarthy's actions.  After six months, he resigned.  The following year, Kennedy wrote a report in which he criticized McCarthy.  In December 1954, the U.S. Senate voted 67 to 22 to condemn McCarthy for his actions.  However, the tide of McCarthyism he had begun lasted into the 1960s.

In 1957, Kennedy became chief counsel on another Senate subcommittee.  This committee was the Senate Select Committee on Improper Activities in the Labor or Management Field.  It was more commonly known as the Rackets Committee.

On this committee, Kennedy investigated corruption in labor unions such as the Teamsters.  The Teamsters Union seeks to protect the working conditions of truck drivers and other workers.  The committee investigated Teamsters president David Beck in 1957.  Beck pled the Fifth Amendment more than a hundred times when questioned.  This cost Beck his position as the union's president.

Kennedy later investigated James R. "Jimmy" Hoffa, who became president of the Teamsters Union after Beck.  Kennedy's work earned him public respect as a determined lawyer.  But he also made enemies of powerful men such as Hoffa.

Opposite page: *Jimmy Hoffa confronts Robert Kennedy during a Rackets Committee meeting.*

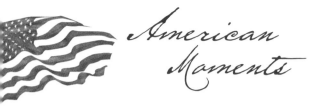

# A POLITICAL FIGURE

In 1959, Kennedy resigned from the Rackets Committee. He went on to lead his brother's campaign for president. In the presidential election, John F. Kennedy ran against Republican candidate Richard M. Nixon. Robert Kennedy helped lead his brother to victory in a close election. In 1961, John Kennedy became the thirty-fifth president of the United States.

*John F. Kennedy (left) and Richard M. Nixon shake hands after the presidential debate.*

President Kennedy appointed Robert attorney general. Many people criticized the appointment. They believed Robert Kennedy only received the position because his brother was president. However, the attorney general quickly proved his worth. He led a tough fight against organized crime. His efforts also led to the conviction of Jimmy Hoffa.

16

*John F. Kennedy (left) and Robert Kennedy stand together shortly after John named Robert attorney general.*

Robert and John Kennedy also worked together to protect the civil rights of African Americans. In the 1950s and 1960s, African Americans fought against discrimination to gain equal rights. This struggle is known as the civil rights movement. Martin Luther King Jr. was a prominent leader of the movement, and received much support from the Kennedys. In 1961, Robert Kennedy sent 400 federal marshals to protect King from a racist mob in Montgomery, Alabama.

17

*Federal troops escort James Meredith* (center) *to registration.*

Kennedy again had to send troops to defend the rights of African Americans in 1962. This time, federal marshals, prison guards, and others protected James Meredith as he registered at the University of Mississippi. The Supreme Court had ruled that Ole Miss must enroll Meredith. However, the school refused to abide by this ruling.

An angry mob descended upon the federal troops when they arrived on September 30. Two people in the mob of 2,000 were killed in the fighting that followed. But, Meredith was able to enroll at the university the following day.

About discrimination Robert Kennedy said, "on this generation of Americans falls the full burden of proving to the world that we really mean it when we say all men are created equal and are equal before the law."

Later, he proposed the Civil Rights Act of 1964. This legislation banned discrimination in voting, jobs, and public places. At this time, many restaurants, hotels, and other public places were segregated. The Civil Rights Act of 1964 made these acts of discrimination unlawful.

Unfortunately, President Kennedy never saw the Civil Rights Act pass. On November 22, 1963, President Kennedy was assassinated in Dallas, Texas. Robert Kennedy was devastated by his brother's sudden death. President Kennedy's death also meant that Vice President Lyndon B. Johnson was now president. Johnson and Robert Kennedy disliked each other, and had a strained working relationship.

Kennedy soon resigned his position as attorney general. He decided to run for the U.S. Senate in New York. He won and started a new chapter in his political career. As a senator, he continued to fight for social reform and civil rights.

Kennedy took a special interest in a poverty-stricken neighborhood in Brooklyn, New York, called Bedford-Stuyvesant, or Bed-Stuy. Most of the people who lived there were African Americans. Many of the residents did not have jobs.

*Lyndon B. Johnson*

John F. Kennedy and his wife, Jacqueline, rode in an open car in a motorcade in Dallas, Texas. It was during this motorcade that John Kennedy was assassinated by Lee Harvey Oswald. Oswald was later shot by Jack Ruby before a trial could be held. To this day, some people believe that Kennedy's and Oswald's deaths were part of a conspiracy. Robert Kennedy privately believed that his enemy Jimmy Hoffa was involved in John's murder. Other groups have thought that the Cuban or Soviet governments had something to do with the crime. Still others believe that John Kennedy was killed by organized crime, or even the U.S. government. However, no sufficient evidence has been found to support any of these theories.

*Robert Kennedy at a U.S. Senate hearing on poverty.*

Families lived in run-down buildings without heat or electricity.

When Kennedy first met the people of Bed-Stuy, they were angry. For ten years, the community had been crying for help, and the government had ignored them. Kennedy made it his mission to bring a better life to these people.

Kennedy went to private businesses for funds. With their help, he established two nonprofit organizations. One was made up of community leaders who decided how Bed-Stuy would be developed and improved. The other group was in charge of raising money to fund the improvements.

Kennedy's aggressive action in Bed-Stuy proved that he was a champion of civil rights. About taking action, he said, "Each time a man stands up for an ideal, or acts to improve the lot of others, or strikes out against injustice, he sends a tiny ripple of hope . . . these ripples will build a current which can sweep down the mightiest walls of oppression and resistance."

President Johnson hands Robert Kennedy pens during the signing of the Civil Rights Act of 1964.

# THE ROAD TO PRESIDENCY

Meanwhile, President Johnson served out the remainder of John Kennedy's term. As president, Johnson continued to support President Kennedy's policies, especially U.S. involvement in the Vietnam War.

In 1964, Johnson ran against Republican candidate Barry Goldwater in the presidential election. Johnson won the election by one of the largest margins in U.S. history. At the time of the election, his approval rating was at 80 percent. However, his approval rating slowly began to decline over his term, mostly due to the Vietnam War.

Vietnam is located in Southeast Asia. This country was once a colony of France. Communist leader Ho Chi Minh led a fight for independence against France. In 1954, the country split into North and South Vietnam. Ho Chi Minh became the communist leader of North Vietnam. Before John Kennedy's presidency, the American government had promised to help protect South Vietnam from communist forces. These forces fought to take control of the South Vietnamese government.

*Ho Chi Minh*

24

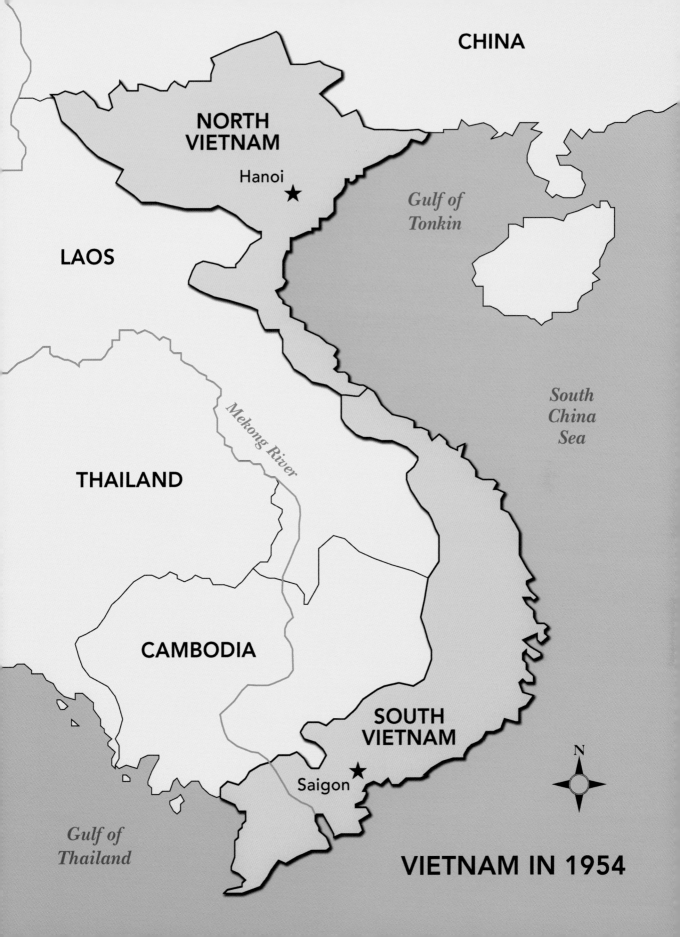

CHINA

NORTH
VIETNAM

Hanoi ★

Gulf of
Tonkin

LAOS

South
China
Sea

Mekong River

THAILAND

CAMBODIA

SOUTH
VIETNAM

Saigon ★

N

Gulf of
Thailand

VIETNAM IN 1954

In the 1960s, the United States became more involved in the Vietnam conflict. The government sent money, weapons, and troops to South Vietnam. However, the war dragged on with little success.

At first, Robert Kennedy supported the presence of U.S. troops in South Vietnam. Later, he became convinced the United States could not win the Vietnam War. In February 1966, Kennedy took a public stand against the war. In a speech, he suggested the United States begin peace talks with the North Vietnamese government. Johnson was outraged that Kennedy would publicly question his judgment. For political reasons, Kennedy decided to keep quiet on Vietnam issues for a while.

A year passed, and Kennedy saw the United States still engaged in a losing battle. He needed to stand up again. On March 2, 1967, Kennedy appeared before the Senate. Kennedy again proposed the United States open peace talks with the North Vietnamese. Once again, Johnson felt betrayed. But Johnson's public support was dwindling. Across the United States, more and more people began protesting the war.

Kennedy considered running for president. He often thought of an inscription on a cigarette case his brother John had given him. It read, "When I'm through, how about you?" After much thought, Kennedy decided it was his turn to lead. On March 16, 1968, he announced his plan to run for president.

Two weeks later, President Johnson appeared in a televised speech that surprised the nation. He announced that he would not run for another term as president. Kennedy's main Democratic opponent would now be Senator Eugene McCarthy from Minnesota.

*Robert Kennedy and Lyndon B. Johnson talk in the Oval Office.*

*Martin Luther King Jr.*

Early in the campaigns, however, the nation was shaken by more shocking news. On April 4, 1968, Martin Luther King Jr. was assassinated in Memphis, Tennessee. King had been fighting for the rights of sanitation workers there. Throughout the United States, African Americans rioted in more than 100 cities. Kennedy visited Coretta Scott King, King's widow, and attended King's funeral.

Kennedy then started a successful campaign. He won the Indiana and Nebraska primaries. But a few days before the California primary, McCarthy won in Oregon. Suddenly, the possibility of defeat stared Kennedy in the face. If he lost the primary, Kennedy knew he'd continue fighting for social justice and racial equality. However, now he needed to work hard for other states' votes.

By the night of the California primary, Kennedy was exhausted from campaigning. Between June 2 and 3, he traveled 1,200 miles (1,931 km) back and forth between San Diego and San Francisco. Along the way, he stopped in numerous cities to campaign. His eyes were bloodshot, and his face looked worn and pale.

During one speech, he became so ill he almost collapsed. But he knew winning the primary would be important. Kennedy did indeed win, only to be killed by Sirhan during his victory celebration.

Kennedy views damage caused by riots in Washington DC.
The riots broke out after the assassination of Martin Luther King, Jr.

Martin Luther King Jr. and his aides stand on the balcony of the Lorraine Motel in Memphis, Tennessee. Starting from the left are Hosea Williams, Jesse Jackson, King, and Ralph Abernathy.

In his years as a civil rights leader, King worked to improve the lives of African Americans. He fought segregation on buses, discrimination in voting, and inequality in schools. Later, King strived to secure better homes and jobs for African Americans. In 1968, King was assassinated while standing on this balcony.

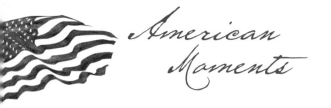

*American Moments*

# ARREST OF SIRHAN

Karl Uecker held Sirhan in a headlock until police arrived on the scene. One of Kennedy's unofficial bodyguards, professional football player Roosevelt Grier, was lying on top of Sirhan. Another man had Sirhan by the legs. When officers entered the room, everyone around Sirhan started shouting, "That's him! That's him!"

People at the scene were hysterical. With the crowd pushing and shoving in all directions, police had difficulty handcuffing the shooter. They feared the angry mob might try to kill Sirhan. Getting him out of the Ambassador Hotel alive would be tricky. The officers also risked being injured or even killed themselves trying to protect him.

Police officers formed a close circle around Sirhan and fought their way out of the building. If people got in the way, they were pushed down. The officers finally got Sirhan safely into a patrol car.

The mob then began rocking the car, hoping to overturn it. Police started swinging their batons to get the angry crowd away from the car. In the car, an officer read Sirhan his rights. "Why did you shoot him?" he asked Sirhan. But Sirhan refused to tell him anything.

At the Rampart Division of the Los Angeles Police Department, Sergeant William Jordan questioned Sirhan. Sirhan refused to give

32

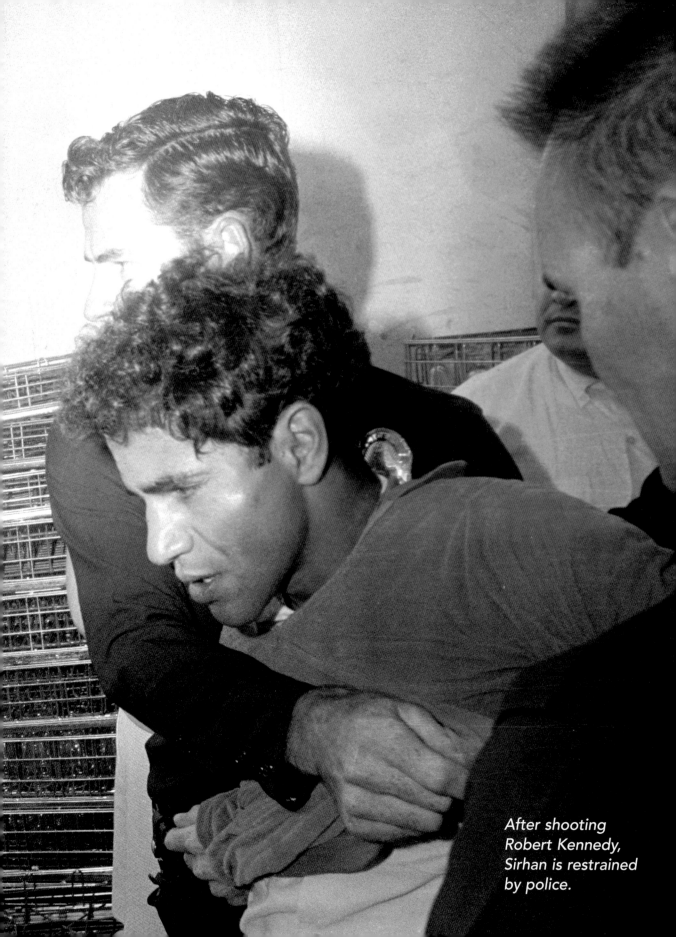

After shooting
Robert Kennedy,
Sirhan is restrained
by police.

his name. Jordan said, "Through fingerprints, you will be identified." But Sirhan continued to be uncooperative. Finally at 2:15 AM on June 5, police booked him as "John Doe." They charged him with assault with intent to commit murder.

Law enforcement officers found a car key in Sirhan's pocket. They began searching the blocks around the Ambassador Hotel for a car that would match the key. At 4:00 PM, police found Sirhan's pink-and-white DeSoto two blocks from the hotel. Inside, they found Sirhan's driver's license. Sirhan's brother Adel also showed up at the police station and confirmed Sirhan's identity.

Meanwhile, doctors at Central Receiving Hospital worked feverishly to save Kennedy's life. When he arrived, he was barely breathing and his heartbeat was weak. Kennedy had been shot four times, but had only three bullet wounds. One of the bullets had passed through his suit coat without touching his body. Kennedy's most serious wound was an inch behind his right ear. The bullet had exploded on impact, creating a serious wound. The other two bullets had entered the senator's right armpit.

Within minutes of arriving, Kennedy stopped breathing. Doctors resuscitated him. His chances of survival looked grim. Kennedy received last rites. Then, doctors transferred him to Good Samaritan Hospital. At 1:44 AM on June 6, Kennedy died, about 26 hours after he was shot. Sirhan was charged with murder.

Kennedy's funeral was held in St. Patrick's Cathedral in New York City, New York. After the funeral, a train carried his body to Arlington National Cemetery outside Washington DC. By the time the train arrived, it was 9:00 PM. Mourners held 1,500 candles during the graveside service. Kennedy was buried near his brother, John.

Robert F. Kennedy Jr. places his hands on his father's coffin. Beside him is Secretary of Health Wilbur Cohen.

It was now time to gather evidence for Sirhan's trial. During a search of Sirhan's home, police found a notebook filled with writing. Sirhan seemed to be obsessed with killing Kennedy. He wrote repeatedly, "RFK must be assassinated." The prosecution believed this was their strongest piece of evidence. The notebook proved Sirhan had intentions of killing the senator.

Sirhan's trial began on January 7, 1969, in the Hall of Justice in Los Angeles. The prosecution and defense tried to strike a deal instead of going to trial. In exchange for Sirhan's guilty plea, the prosecution offered life imprisonment. This deal would save Sirhan from a possible death sentence. The judge, however, declined the plea bargain. He believed the public deserved the truth, and that the truth would come out during the trial.

The defense then tried to convince the jury that Sirhan was mentally ill when he committed the murder. If they could prove Sirhan was unstable, he might not receive a death sentence. The trial lasted 15 weeks. After three days of deliberation, the jury returned a guilty verdict. On April 23, the jury voted that Sirhan should be put to death in the gas chamber.

Surprisingly, the Kennedy family was not happy about the sentence. They did not want to see Sirhan put to death. Kennedy's brother, Edward, wrote a letter to the judge stating, "My brother was a man of love and sentiment and compassion. He would not have wanted his death to be a cause for the taking of another life." In 1972, California's law allowing the death penalty was ruled unconstitutional. Consequently, Sirhan's death sentence was changed to life in prison.

# FIVE WOUNDED

Sirhan Bishara Sirhan shot five other people that night at the Ambassador Hotel. They all survived. Campaign worker Paul Schrade was four to five feet (1–1.5 m) behind Kennedy. He fell backward, shot in the head. At the time of the shooting, his eyes were fixed on the senator, who had just finished shaking hands with a busboy.

Photo taken after Sirhan's arrest

Irwin Stroll, a seventeen-year-old student and campaign worker, was shot in the left leg. Nineteen-year-old Continental News Service reporter Ira Goldstein was shot stepping over the wounded Stroll. He remembered feeling a sharp pain in his left hip and falling against a wall.

William Weisel, an ABC-TV unit manager was shot in the abdomen. Forty-two-year-old Elizabeth Evans, a close friend of Kennedy's aide Pierre Salinger, bent down to pick up a lost shoe. One of the bullets grazed her forehead. After the shooting stopped, she heard someone scream that a woman had been shot. She did not even realize it was her until she felt blood running down her face.

# A CHANGED AMERICA

The United States changed after the assassination of Robert F. Kennedy. Many people believed Kennedy would win the Democratic nomination for president. Kennedy's rival for the nomination, Eugene McCarthy, lost support after the California primary. These events opened the door for U.S. Senator Hubert Humphrey of Minnesota to take the nomination.

During the 1968 election, American involvement in Vietnam was a hot issue. Many Americans wanted the United States to pull out of the war. Robert Kennedy and Eugene McCarthy were "peace candidates." They felt the United States should handle the Vietnam situation differently. Hubert Humphrey was a pro-war candidate. Humphrey won the presidential nomination at the Democratic National Convention in Chicago, Illinois, in August 1968. This made many antiwar Americans unhappy.

Antiwar protesters in Chicago took to the streets. They rioted for five days. The Chicago police, the army, the National

*Hubert Humphrey*

*Antiwar protesters use park benches as a barricade to block police during the Democratic National Convention.*

Guard, and even the FBI tried to stop the riot. In total, about 28,000 law enforcement members spread through the streets. They used tear gas, mace, and physical force to break up the crowds. In the chaos, police injured many protesters, reporters, and bystanders.

The police violence in Chicago changed the attitude of many protesters. They saw the law as an enemy from which they must defend themselves. The first war protests, which started in 1965, were nonviolent demonstrations. Most of these protests took place on university campuses. But situations between protesters and police became tense as the government sent more troops to Vietnam.

*Richard M. Nixon*

In the 1968 presidential election, Humphrey ran against Nixon. During the campaign, Nixon claimed to have a secret plan to end the Vietnam War. This time, Nixon won a close election to become president.

One of the most violent protests took place on May 4, 1970, at Kent State University in Ohio. The protest happened just days after President Nixon announced a full-scale bombing of Cambodia. Until this time, Cambodia had stayed neutral during the Vietnam War. But many believed that North Vietnamese forces were hiding there. News of the bombing upset many antiwar activists. It seemed to them that the war was going to get worse, not better. Students at Kent State gathered to protest the attack.

On May 4, the Ohio National Guard ordered the students to stop protesting and leave the campus commons. When they refused, guardsmen moved in to break up the rally. Some protesters shouted angrily and threw rocks.

At some point, the guardsmen fired. The demonstrators were unarmed. Four students were killed and nine more wounded during the thirteen seconds of gunfire. No one is certain why the guardsmen fired on the students. To this day, it is a matter of controversy.

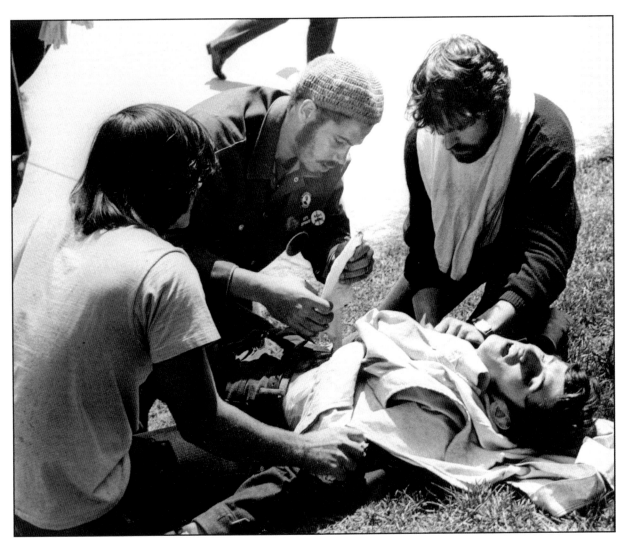

*Students give first aid to a wounded fellow student at Kent State.*

The increasingly violent antiwar protests put pressure on Nixon to end the war. In June 1969, Nixon proposed a policy that promised the gradual withdrawal of American troops from Vietnam.

Americans will never know how Kennedy would have addressed the Vietnam War if he had survived. But he will be remembered for the great work he did while living. Kennedy was a true defender of civil rights and of the poor. With Kennedy's death, the United States lost a great leader and champion of social justice and equality.

41

# TIMELINE

**1925** On November 20, Robert Francis Kennedy is born.

**1950** On June 17, Kennedy marries Ethel Skakel.

**1951** Kennedy manages his brother John's successful campaign for U.S. Senate.

**1953** Kennedy serves on the U.S. Senate Permanent Subcommittee on Investigations. This committee is headed by Senator Joseph McCarthy and investigates accused communists.

**1953 to 1975** The Vietnam War is fought between North Vietnam and South Vietnam. The United States sends troops to support South Vietnam.

**1957** Kennedy serves on the Senate Select Committee on Improper Activities and looks into corruption in labor unions.

**1959** Kennedy manages John F. Kennedy's presidential campaign.

**1961** John F. Kennedy becomes president. He appoints Robert Kennedy U.S. attorney general.

**1963** On November 22, President Kennedy is assassinated in Dallas, Texas.

Kennedy resigns as attorney general and wins a New York seat in the U.S. Senate.

**1964** The Civil Rights Act of 1964 that Kennedy recommended is passed. This act bans discrimination in public places.

**1968** On March 16, Kennedy announces his campaign for presidency.

On April 4, Martin Luther King Jr. is assassinated.

On June 4, Kennedy wins the California Democratic primary. He is shot by Sirhan Bishara Sirhan at the Ambassador Hotel in Los Angeles an hour later.

On June 6, Kennedy dies at Good Samaritan Hospital.

In August, Hubert Humphrey wins the Democratic primary in Chicago, Illinois. Antiwar protesters riot.

**1969** Sirhan is sentenced to death. This sentence is later changed to life in prison.

**1970** On May 4, four students are killed and nine are wounded in an antiwar riot at Kent State University in Ohio.

*American Moments*

# FAST FACTS

When going home from work one night, Robert F. Kennedy saw a light on in James R. Hoffa's office. Kennedy said, "If he's still at work, we ought to be." He and his coworker went back to the office and worked for another two hours. After hearing of this, Hoffa delighted in leaving his office light on at night.

At 43, Kennedy's brother, John, was the youngest president ever elected. If he had been elected president in 1968, Kennedy would have been 42 years old, beating his brother's record.

On July 30, 1975, Hoffa disappeared from a restaurant in Detroit, Michigan. He was never seen again, and it is believed that he was murdered. In 1982, he was officially declared dead, though his body has never been found.

The Ambassador Hotel has been closed for more than ten years. Today, many movie productions are filmed there. In the 1994 comedy *The Mask*, the Coco Bongo nightclub was filmed in the old Ambassador Cocoanut Grove club. The kitchen pantry, however, is boarded up and off-limits to visitors.

All of the physical evidence from Kennedy's assassination trial is on file at the state archives in Sacramento, California. The items include Sirhan's blue shirt and the gun he used to kill Kennedy. Another private collection of items exists at the University of Massachusetts Dartmouth Library in the Robert F. Kennedy Assassination Archives.

# WEB SITES
# WWW.ABDOPUB.COM

Would you like to learn more about the Assassination of Robert F. Kennedy? Please visit **www.abdopub.com** to find up-to-date Web site links about the Assassination of Robert F. Kennedy and other American moments. These links are routinely monitored and updated to provide the most current information available.

*Robert Kennedy shakes hands with schoolchildren in Mechanicville, New York.*

# GLOSSARY

assassinate: to murder a very important person.

attorney general: the chief law officer of a national or state
government.

civil rights: the individual rights of a citizen, such as the right to vote
or freedom of speech.

communism: a social and economic system in which everything is
owned by the government and given to the people as needed.

counsel: a lawyer or group of lawyers who give legal advice.

defense: the lawyer or lawyers who represent the accused person in
criminal cases. The accused person is known as the defendant.

Democrat: a member of the Democratic Party. Democrats believe in
social change and strong government.

discrimination: treating a group of people unfairly based on
characteristics such as race, class, or gender.

Fifth Amendment: part of the Bill of Rights. This amendment says a
citizen must be paid for property taken by the government. It also
says a citizen cannot be punished without due process of law, tried
twice for the same crime, or forced to testify against himself in court.
A person who refuses to testify against himself is said to be "taking
the Fifth."

incriminate: to charge or present evidence of involvement in a crime.

intellectual: someone who is very knowledgeable.

labor unions: a group formed to help workers receive their rights.

last rites: a Catholic ritual in which a priest prays for a dying person.

McCarthyism: accusing people of being disloyal to their country by saying that they are communist.

nonprofit organization: an organization set up for charity or education instead of for profit.

plea bargain: an agreement between lawyers in a court case in which the accused person is allowed to plead guilty to a lesser crime.

prosecution: the lawyer or lawyers who represent the government in criminal cases.

Republican: a member of the Republican Party. Republicans believe in individual responsibility and small government.

segregation: to put social or political barriers around certain groups of people based on characteristics such as race, class, or gender.

unconstitutional: something that goes against the laws of the U.S. Constitution.

# INDEX